SHELTER IN THIS PLACE

Meditations on 2020

MEG RILEY, EDITOR

SKINNER HOUSE BOOKS

BOSTON

skinnerhouse.org

Printed in the United States

Cover design by Kathryn Sky-Peck
Text design by Jeff Miller

print ISBN: 978-1-55896-872-1
eBook ISBN: 978-1-55896-873-8

5 4 3 2 1
25 24 23 22 21

Cataloging-in-Publication data on file with the
Library of Congress

"We Cannot Escape Each Other" by Manish Mishra-Marzetti
was previously published in the UUA Braver/Wiser series,
April 15, 2020.

CONTENTS

INTRODUCTION

One of the greatest blessings of being part of a spiritual community, even one that is loosely woven, is that our own experiences loop into those of other people's over and over. We're not all having the same pandemic, but because of the connections of Unitarian Universalism, we can know how it's going for other people with other lives.

Newspapers give us sobering statistics about how the Covid pandemic impacts particular communities, how BIPOC folks suffer and die the most, how the elderly and the incarcerated are trapped in dangerous environments, how the infection rates in cities and states and countries rise and fall.

But it's the heart-spoken words of people we are connected to, people both known and unknown to us, that keep us human, that resonate with our own pain and joy, strength and despair.

This anthology from Unitarian Universalists about their pandemic experiences is offered as a testament to our collective grit and grief, rage and resistance, love and loneliness. The readings come from a variety of perspectives, identities, and geographies and were written throughout the long year.

And what a year it's been! The voices in this anthology reinforce for me why I am grateful and well nourished as part of the Unitarian Universalist faith. These are not sugar-coated or superficial prayers: they are

the honest utterances of human hearts. In a world
of half-truths and lies, it is a balm to be genuine with
each other.

Many of the authors question the very notion of
prayer itself. As Roger Butts writes, "If praying is your
thing, go ahead and pray. . . . Thank a nurse, if you'd
like to do something a bit more concrete." KJ Walker
begins her piece, "I want to pray for you, but I don't
know how."

Call it prayer, call it honest reflection, call it poetry.
These writers speak from their hearts, summoning
words from the deepest places. They express faith that
is personal and collective, grounded and full of longing.
Authentic faith. As Ali Bell-Delgado writes, "Not the
faith of fairytales and limited understanding. / Not the
faith that these things will change somehow without our
doing the work of change. / Help us dig deeper into our
faith in humanity."

These writers share a profound belief in the power of
serving their communities. Emily DeTar writes, "Faith
is leaving behind / the God everyone else says / will be
there for you and / showing up for people anyway." Mya
Sophia Wade-Harper commits to "holding up as much
brick as I can to keep those I love alive."

In 2020, Unitarian Universalists grieved the omni-
present pandemic of racism in the United States. Arif
Mamdani and Ruth McKenzie, praying in Minneapolis
just blocks and days from the vicious murder of George
Floyd, declare that "what we truly feel is rage, is a

longing for the sharp knives of judgment to be wielded, for justice to cut out the heart of white supremacy, to cut out a system that takes our breath away." Margalie Belizaire longs "to get to a safer space for Black bodies." As Manish Mishra-Marzetti writes, "nothing has been untouched: my nation / my community / me, myself / all of us turned inside out."

These pages hold many kinds of anguish: survivors whose loved ones died alone, essential workers facing fear and risk, parents raising their children in isolation. "Grief wears so many faces," Holly Mueller writes. Kathleen Wade folds laundry, wishing she was "forty years younger and able to march . . . folding in layers of sorrow and sorting out rage." JeKaren Olaoya reminds us, "Don't forget to mourn. . . . Mourn / Until your chest / Unclenches / And breath / Eases."

My deep hope is that this collection of writings allows each one of us to know that, even in the separateness of our masked and socially distanced grief, we are not mourning alone. May the companionship of these writers' words allow us to unclench and our breath to ease.

For despite all of the anguish, grief, loss, rage, and struggle, the writers describe resilience and joy. They take solace in the birth of ducklings and the unfurling of new leaves. They persevere, as Megan Lloyd Joiner writes, "piecing things together one moment at a time." Alex Klingenberg affirms that "I'm pretty sure we're doing alright . . . even though I've worn the same / sweatshirt for six days straight."

Daniel Kanter reminds us that "the goodness of life is ours if we look deeply for it / and give thanks for what we have and who we have it with." Margalie Belizaire enjoins us to "give our all to this / and hold nothing back / for precious lives depend on it."

Because finally, as Danielle Di Bona tells us, "We have survived. We are not the same, yet we have survived, battered and bruised. It is a good day."

I am grateful to share this precious faith with you. May this book contain words that heal, comfort, and inspire you in the days ahead. Thanks be to all who contributed their writings and to the wonderful folks at Skinner House Books, especially Mary Benard and Larisa Hohenboken.

Meg Riley
January 2021

THE BIRDS WILL SING

Daniel C. Kanter

People are staying home
and the days are passing now as we watch and wait
and hope for reprieve from this house arrest.
And we pray for the health for all,
the love of one another,
to see the goodness in ourselves and our families,
and the blessings of life.
And meanwhile, as we slow our feverish consumption,
the birds sing a little louder, the earth eases its breath,
and we can sense the faint blessings in all this mess.
The goodness of life is ours if we look deeply for it
and give thanks for what we have and who we have it with.
Amen. Hope resides in us, and love abounds . . .
Let us sing.

THE NURSE AND THE HANDMADE MASK, WITH HAIR TIES

Joanne M. Giannino

She made this for him:
my son, an EMT
transferring her patient
from the nursing home
to the ER.

As he left,
with his new patient
carefully covered
and strapped in
for safety
on his stretcher,

She pushed the mask,
handmade with hair ties,
into his pocket.

Like an auntie
stuffs a five-dollar bill
in your pocket
before you leave for home
so you can get yourself
a little something,

Or a grandmother
insists you take
the leftovers
when you go.

Love in a fiver,
your heart in
a casserole
to reheat later.

She said,
"Take care."

TELLING YOU NOW

Jason Cook

I love you.

I forgot to tell you
the last time I saw you
on the street as you waved goodbye.
A barely registered moment,
you in jeans and your hair messed up
and me in that jacket from the thrift store.

But it's the ball I remember,
the military ball
where you took me as your date.
How did you dare to?
Way back then?

How they stared when we walked in—
You in your uniform
and me in my tuxedo.
Someone thought I was a waiter.

You had on white gloves and we danced,
though I am not a good dancer
even when I'm not nervous like I was that night
as the whispers swirled in the air around us.

And later, when it was all over,
we stood under a starry sky like an old movie backdrop.

You pressing into my hand a button from your jacket,
a gold button with a military insignia on it.

And I still have it.

I love you.
I forgot to tell you then,
so I'm telling you now.
Even though you are gone,
stolen by AIDS.

There is a new virus in town,
I'd tell you now, if you were here.
A new thing to wrestle and fear.
And so much of it is terrible.

But it has reminded me of one thing:
to say what's important
while I can, when I can.
Because I may not always have the chance.
You taught me that first
and every fiber of my being is reminded of it now.

I love you.
I was scared to tell you then,
so I'm telling you now.
Because *now*—even though it's not what we expected—
is precious
and it may be all we have.

REMEMBERING

Eileen Casey-Campbell

Cut off from my beloveds,
the ones whose faces
and laughs and little gestures
I know as well as my own,
I am relearning,
remembering
the names of the beloveds
I had somehow
long forgotten.

Wild carrot, bitter dock,
smooth sumac, plantain,
I remember you.
Your shape, your scent,
the way you gesture to me
on the roadside,
along the trails
I've walked without looking
for so long.

Black caps, elderberries,
chokecherries,
now I recall
your shyness,
as you peek out
from underneath your neighbors.

Walnuts and butternuts,
I know you.
I remember your generosity,
how you drop abundance
in my lap
though I haven't lifted
my eyes to your branches
in ages.

There is so much
purposeful forgetting
I and my ancestors
have done.
So much we have buried
too deep in our bones
to be heard.
So much we have cut
out of our hearts
in order to live
with ourselves.

My beloveds,
I am remembering you.
You are piecing
me back together again.

BREAKFAST, CHAOS, BEDTIME

Lisa Doege

Very early on, as the pandemic took hold in the United States, I wrote the following schedule on the parsonage kitchen whiteboard one day: *breakfast – chaos – bedtime*.

I had, for the first eight days or so of no school and ten or more of social distancing, been dutifully posting a detailed schedule every day. I knew that both residents of the parsonage thrive on structure (and also resist it). I'd consumed a million pieces of internet advice, suggestions, warnings, and ideas. I'd paid attention to what pastors and parents on the West Coast were saying about life further along into the pandemic than we were in the Midwest. I'd been operating on the theory that it's easier to start structured and loosen up than to start loose and attempt to impose structure later.

But that day I couldn't do it. I could neither predict nor decide what our day would hold, other than a beginning and an ending and a whole lot of chaos in between. I'd done my best to hold chaos at bay, but here it was, even as on that very day the Surgeon General of the United States was saying, "It's going to get bad this week."

A few days earlier I had written, "The first significant lesson of this time, for me, is that doing things the right way no longer means following the recipe as written." The second significant lesson, I was learning, was that I must let the chaos be chaos. Order and schedules would emerge. Order and schedules that make sense for this time. Order and schedules that I could neither impose nor even conceive from my pre-pandemic mind-set. My job as pastor, as parent, as person, is to let that happen. To trust that it will happen and to have faith that it will contain blessings beyond my limited apprehension.

This is when I should be writing an Easter and/or Passover newsletter column. When I should be finding metaphors to remind us all that personal Good Fridays and Easters, personal Passovers and Exoduses, come into each of our lives. That the Biblical stories grew out of a need to make sense of human experience and that, far from being imposed by external authority, the holy days are organic reflections and celebrations of those lived experiences. This year instead I'll just say: there is chaos in the Easter story along with celebration. There is chaos in the Passover story along with celebration.

And there will be celebration in our pandemic story, along with chaos, when the time comes to make of this time in our lives a story.

THE SERMON

Martha Kirby Capo

I cannot sing with you, my people,
but I can sing *to* you, I can sing
for you across the viscous
Silence settling Her thick Self
into sixty thousand mostly empty cubic feet.
She is become *ruah*. She buoys
my voice, helps me fill the aching
spaces between us; She links us
as an ocean connecting islands, our
lonely little shells dancing along
the interdependent strands.

(Pick us up; put us to your ear;
listen. "We're still here," we roar
inside our small and fragile spaces.)

Still, I mourn the chairs
we no longer have a need for
stacked like pillars of salt
against the walls on
Sunday morning.

IN THE COVID-19 LAB

Chalice L. Gustaveson

Each biohazard bag, a sample
Each sample, a name
Each name, a person
Each person, a loved one

For each loved one, a prayer:
May you be negative
May you be healthy
May you be safe

WE CANNOT ESCAPE ONE ANOTHER

Manish Mishra-Marzetti

An invisible virus without any cure; a death sentence for some and not for others. This is all too familiar to me, as a gay man who came out, at the age of twenty in the early 1990s, prior to the advent of effective treatments for HIV. It felt like the possibility of the disease dominated every aspect of my existence in those tender days.

Summoning the courage to share my truth with loved ones was invariably greeted with the reaction, "Please stay safe. We don't want you to die." The reminders were unnecessary. In the gay community, seized by the desire to survive, we were encouraged to assume that anyone we met could be asymptomatic, carrying the disease without knowing that they were HIV-positive.

Every exploratory human connection, every kiss, every expression of love resulted in an insistent anxiety: How safe had I been? Was it safe enough? The only 100 percent guarantee of safety was complete abstinence, which would require sacrificing intimacy altogether.

Fear can have its own exponential curve, as anxiety and reality collide. My first few months of being a "new gay" were greeted with the death of an older cousin. His family was too scared to admit that he died of AIDS and I was too scared to tell him, in our final conversation, that I was also gay.

Echoes of the past fill my present. I scan the grocery store aisle: is anyone sneezing or coughing, or otherwise looking unwell? Is the aisle too crowded? Maybe it's safer to wait or come back another day. Anxiety, both familiar and new, silently fills the air, distrust finely woven through it. A new disease, without any cure, is pushing us apart.

And yet we cannot escape one another. We need each other. Whether I acknowledge it or not, the guarantee of safety does not exist. We buy groceries: we touch products and surfaces that others have touched; we breathe the air that has touched the lungs of others.

At the store, an older woman asks my husband for help; she cannot read the small print on the label of a product she needs. He leans in and reads it out loud for her. Inches apart, inches too close, inches and feet embodying love and our shared sense of humanity.

May our abiding commitment to Love be the thing we cannot escape.

PLANS

Megan Lloyd Joiner

My spouse will not travel to Vienna in June.
We will not return to our ancestors' land in July.

This child will meet her grandparents
    and aunt and uncle and cousins
when she is a bouncing baby girl

no longer rich with milk breath
her newborn glow long gone.

The friends who were coming will not come.
The plans we'd made do not matter now.

The birds still sing; flowers bloom.
The owl hoots, and my soul remembers.

Piecing things together
one moment at a time.

THE LONG DAY

Mya Sophia Wade-Harper

Regret pinches at my veins
Tears clawing at my eyes
Sorrow etched to the bone
It is the pain of this moment,
The pain of those all around me suffering
The want to do something!
The shock
And I, in a daze, move on
I capture the joy in the small butterflies that mark
my path
I store it inside till the tears come out
And when they do, I sing till my eyes dry
No matter my pain, I must move on—though my
pace has no merit
I watch as the world crumbles, holding up as much
brick as I can to keep those I love alive
And it's enough
More than enough

A PRAYER FOR GOING FORWARD

Jamie W. Johnson

Spirit of Life, as I put on this mask, please

Bless this face, which has been covered in fabric, in plastic, in tears.

Bless this mind, filled with worries and fears, statistics and new words, policies and predictions. May our memories and our dreams bring comfort.

Bless these eyes that have seen suffering not only from the virus but also from violence. Give us the focus to stay turned towards hope and bending the arc of justice.

Bless these ears that have been rubbed raw by the elastic of masks, by daily harrowing news reports, by the cries of neighbors. Please balance this with the joyous sounds of singing together again soon.

Bless each living breath, made so much more difficult by the virus and the knee on the neck. May our breathing be easy, may it be clear. May we not be suffocated.

As I wash my hands,

Bless these that hands that have worked essentially, helped generously. We have worried about everything we've touched, feared the contagion they might carry. How precious is innocent human touch. We know now that we took it for granted.

Bless these arms, for "hug hunger" is real. We have missed holding our loved ones, particularly those who left us too soon. Our collective shoulders ache from the grief we carry, along with the protest signs.

As I go forth, please

Bless these legs, which have carried us so far, and still carry us. Please give us the power to keep on moving forward.

Bless this heart, for it hurts. Damaged by the virus, racing from fear, aching for each other. The joy we feel, the love, has grown stronger too. May our hearts stay true and strong.

Bless us, Spirit of Life, so that we may begin to know relief and healing from the trauma wrought this year.

Amen.

SHELTERED IN PLACE

Lisa Nosal

As we navigate our world as it is now, this strange and unfamiliar world where we must physically distance ourselves from each other and shelter in place: Let us remember the trees.

Let's root ourselves like they do. Standing separately, yes, but with our roots reaching down into the earth and stretching out until they meet and intertwine with the roots of our neighbors.

Let's shelter each other like they do. Reaching our branches up into the sky and stretching out until we can sense—not touch, just sense—our neighbors' branches, where they can start dancing together in the wind.

We stand in a grove, separate but connected. Our roots entangled with each other, our leaves whispering with each other.

We grow rooted in our communities, drawing wisdom up from the earth, this land, this home. We draw up the wisdom of those who have tended this land for millennia, who know the meaning of this place.

We extend up into the sky, inviting the wisdom of those who live in the branches. Wisdom from the feet and claws and feathers and fur of those who have lived and played here, who have found shelter and community here. All those, past and present, seen and hidden, who shelter in this place with us. Who find shelter in this place with us.

Let us tap into the wisdom of trees during this time. Let us live into the meaning of deep community and radical connection even as we are seemingly separated. Let us grow our connections so deep into the earth and so wide into the canopy that we know, like the trees, that we are not alone. We are never alone.

Let us remember we are all sheltered and connected by the sky.

PORTAL

Emily Wright-Magoon

"The pandemic is a portal." —ARUNDHATI ROY

Has this ever happened to you? You move from where you are to go get something in the next room. Maybe you're looking for the TV remote or about to make a snack. You walk through the doorway and suddenly you have completely forgotten what you were looking for.

Psychologists call this the doorway effect. Walking through open doors, crossing a threshold, resets the memory to make room for the creation of a new episode.

We are currently passing through many doorways. We are facing a pandemic unseen in any of our lifetimes. We are deepening our reckoning with our country's history of slavery and colonization, of white supremacy and the devaluing of Black and brown lives. In your personal life, you may also be moving across a threshold: the death of a loved one, the loss of a job, a diagnosis, a searching question. . . .

The key concept in the doorway effect is to *make room*. As we move over the threshold, that reset jars us, making space to leave behind our outworn ideas and practices and birth something new.

But that possibility is only available to us if we are open to it. Change is something that happens to us. But transition and transformation—those are internal and relational. Unless we make room for something new, unless we allow ourselves to be reoriented, no real change happens. We just find the remote and go back to our show.

To cross that threshold ready for transformation, what in us—in our lives, in our relationships, in our world—needs to shift?

Let us cross this threshold ready to reckon with our country's legacy of brutality and white supremacy, ready to rumble with deep change, ready to radically reorient our world into a place where interdependence is not taken for granted or squandered.

Don't just grab the remote. Let's move through the portal instead.

A PRAYER FOR YOU

KJ Walker

I want to pray for you,
but I don't know how.
I desperately
scream at my ancestors:
This isn't okay!
I can feel the tears brim in their eyes
behind me,
holding me up.

I want to pray
for your pain,
for your struggle.
I want to bless all of it away,
but I can't find the right words
to wash away your fear,
to wash away
the way you hold yourself
up so stiffly.
I want to pray bended knee to something,
anything.
Whispering,
repeating
begging
words for change.

Yet words fail
what I want them to do
Who to pray to

But today
I hold you in my heart,
light the candle,
and ask them
to bless your body and spirit,
to hold you up
as I would hold you up.
Tonight, I pray for you.
Tonight, I witness your pain.
Please, just know that I love you.

REVERENCE

Peg Duthie

The teachers I have trusted the most
each have confessed to asking God
What in the hell . . . ? throughout their lives
while keeping hold of their books and faith.

Small wonder how slippery
Thou shalt not kill
becomes in the palms
of people with power to lose,

for see how many first and only children
God slew across the land
to make some point,
not to mention Isaac's near-miss.

They who see themselves as gods
insist that our children belong
in schools and stores and crowds,
even as the virus
tests how much and how much more we can bear—

"Thou shalt not kill"? *Thou shalt have no other gods—*
not teachers and not presidents.
Tables have been turned and overturned
in temples throughout my world, and I
will not cease asking *What in the hell . . . ?*
no matter how grateful I am to still be alive.

NECESSARY MERCIES

Emily DeTar Birt

I believe in naps,
a glass of cold water,
long showers,
mango slices
beading juice on your tongue,
daydreaming while everyone else meditates.

We were made for grace.
Not for perfectionism or productivity,
but for wet cloths on fevered temples,
for layered cakes,
for the person who holds the door
or pays for our groceries.

Grace is the only way
we all get out alive.

GIVING LOVE THE LAST WORD

Tara K. Humphries

It is becoming so clear, isn't it, that heartbreak and beauty are both true, sometimes even at the same time.

Last week, listening to the latest pandemic statistics on the news, I learned of the murder of Ahmaud Arbery, a twenty-five-year-old Black man shot and killed by two white men while out running in Georgia in late February. Heartbreaking doesn't begin to cover it.

That same morning, I met up with a close friend for a run. Sun shining, it was warm enough for shorts and T-shirts. We turned in and out of neighborhoods, hit the local park and river trail, impatiently waited at innumerable crosswalks . . . all the while talking and laughing and breathing deeply, moving our bodies on a spring day out in the world. A celebration of friendship, of health, and of life. What a gift.

Yet there remained a heaviness to that morning. She is Black. And we are both twenty-five. I am aware each morning that we step into a world that sees us differently. I run with privilege I did not earn; she runs with fear she does not deserve. And I know I cannot protect her from people who look like me.

If you pay attention, this world will break your heart.

But then there is the beauty. The sunshine and the birdsong, the green grass and the story sharing and the *laughter*. Oh my God, the laughter. Sometimes I have to stop on those runs, laughing so hard I'm doubled over with my hands on my knees. "Laughter," as author Ann Lamott says, "is carbonated holiness." Those shared moments of movement and friendship out on a fresh morning in a dangerous world are not just beautiful—they are holy.

If heartbreak is where we stop, then perhaps we're not paying attention at all.

The truth is that fear and bravery hold hands. The holy and the lifegiving exist alongside the terror and injustice of our world. Death and life are in a constant dance. We can do more than resist white supremacy; we can celebrate Black *life*.

And perhaps in listening, hearing, and *believing* the stories and experiences of people who hold different identities than we do, we can allow our hearts to break so that we might feel them open. For it is with hearts that can hold the harsh reality of pain and racism and death that we might be moved to that deeper truth: that life, beauty, and the transformative power of Love will, indeed, have the last word.

ABOUT PEOPLE

Jami A. Yandle

Recently, a friend asked me how many deaths I had
    witnessed
as a healthcare chaplain
working through a pandemic.
I told them the truth:
that I stopped counting the number of bodies
I helped move to a gurney
a long time ago
because the numbers are not healthy for me to think
    about.

And anyway,
the important thing about people is all the good stuff
in the details that remain in our heart
when the body moves on.
This is what matters most,
in my opinion.
For it is the heart that echoes back to us
the memory of their unique laugh,
or their love of flowers,
or their spirit on fire for justice,
or the way they showed up for their community,
children, family, friends, and pets,
for instance.

These are the attributes I remember,
that make people a person to me.
And when we are missing a person,
it means we are missing a friend,
a family member (chosen and blood),
god forbid a child, or a beloved partner.
These memories are infinite
and should not
be reduced to black-and-white numbers
on some random graph, chart, or checklist
conjured out of morbid curiosity—
to prove just what, exactly?

NOT ALONE

Linnea Nelson

I didn't want you to be alone.
Not when there are so many who love you
and want to be with you.

I didn't want you to be hooked up to machines,
with anxious nurses staring
out of scared eyes and

peering into your room
less often than you needed.
I didn't want you to be alone.

But you must know:

I was with you
as you took your final breaths
and passed to the other side.

I called on peace
to be there with you.
Love to surround you.
I was there and you were not alone.

MYRSKY TULEE (THE STORM COMES)

Manish Mishra-Marzetti

The storm comes,
    churning all that has been in its path;
    washing away the molted husks
        of shrimplings
    and, in its place
    tossing wood, seaweed, and feathers
        carelessly onto the shore.

I sit amidst the debris,
    as observer,
    as that which has also been churned,
    because, truly,
        nothing has been untouched:
        my nation
        my community
        me, myself
    all of us turned inside out.

Centuries, if not millennia, of
    conquest and domination,
        in the name of being
        "a favored people"
    exposed,
        like wreckage,
    lying naked in the sand.

Many look away.
The lies that have been written,
    histories and mythos bleeding into one,
    conflated national epics and self-perceptions,
        mask an insecurity
        that no modest reform will heal;
The lies that have been believed,
    that we have taught others,
        perpetuating harm so profound
        that a whole life's work
        can feel like
nothing.

Easier to deny, for some,
    that there is a storm—
        after all,
        don't all storms eventually pass?
So ephemeral, so temporary.

I sit with the flotsam,
    yearning for the illusion of order
        that preceded upheaval—
but this is not that time.

I am part of the ecosystem that
    gave us the lies.
And I have also been a harbinger
    of the storm.

I sit now
   in its wake.
Looking fully at the myths and untruths
   laid bare.
That which feels "ugly,"
   churned and in disarray,
   holds the promise of
new life.

Note: "The storm comes" is a direct translation of the Finnish phrase "myrsky tulee," a language the author speaks and a land and people that are kin to him. This Finnish phrase was a direct inspiration for this reflection.

COULD WE TALK ABOUT

Anne Barker

Could we talk about
the dissonance
between what we teach our children
and how we live our lives?

Could we talk about
sharing
and how we don't?

Could we talk about
the ways that privilege
binds us
to suffering,

the ways that suffering
starves us
of freedom,

the ways that freedom
isn't
freedom
and never was?

Could we talk about
love?

THE BEAST OF MIND

Richard Baydin

Nobody can get near me.
I am wrapped up in distance,
in terror, in despair, in rage
Why can't anyone help me, hope me, find me?
I am lost in the world.
My words are chopped up—capsized—nickled—
there are mountains covering me.
I am mute and mummified,
so scared and lost in my thoughts.
Grief blocks the tears,
opens the gates to monsoons
Suffering has no end
Broken to pieces
Go out to nowhere
Go out to brokenness
Go out to unrelatedness
Go out to darkness
Go out in the furthermost reaches of weeping
Only God's world is a place for me to sit
Only God is big enough to squeeze me tight

GOD IS SLEEPING ON THE COUCH TONIGHT

Emily DeTar Birt

People are told
faith gives you comfort.

This is faith too:
Processing the pain
. . . or not.

Washing yet another set of dishes
as the world gets ready to collapse
into the sun,
or into death
after death
after death . . .

God and I are not on speaking terms.
I no longer know what to believe,
and that is faith too.

What is mercy
when you're on the phone
with someone who just lost
their husband,
their child's father,
with no way to touch them
as they died?

The Holy can sort this out
in a Bible verse some other day.

Faith is leaving behind
the God everyone else says
will be there for you and
showing up for people anyway.

DON'T FORGET TO MOURN

JeKaren Olaoya

Don't forget to mourn
Properly,
The way you don't want anyone to see
Wailing
Thrashing
Heaving
With each breath
Releasing
Purging

Mourn
All that you have lost,
Who you have lost,
Both
In passing over
And through,
Leaving behind an emptiness
That draws up
And squeezes heartily

Mourn
With no regard to
Place
Or time
Feeling deeply
The etching of each second

Across bare skin
Leaving behind
Canyons
To fill

Mourn
Until eyes,
Bleary and aching,
Strain to see

Mourn
Until your chest
Unclenches
And breath
Eases

Mourn
Until your spirit
Sighs
With relief,
Settles and snores

Mourn

PROTEST IN THE LAUNDRY ROOM

Kathleen Wade

I am folding my husband's shirts,
smoothing the seams. I am
falling apart at the seams. I am
shaking the wrinkles from towels.
I am shaking inside. Can you tell?
Does it show? I wish I were forty
years younger and able to march.
I am longing to take a stand.
I stand instead in the laundry room
measuring liquid detergent,
pouring it into the tray while
a thousand young people holding
their flashlight phones in the air
in DC's Lafayette Square sing
"Lean on Me." I am leaning over
the sorting table letting my tears
fall on my husband's shirts. I sway
and lean with the young, in the
only way I can—the way I've done
everything—virtually—since
the middle of March (since
this deadly virus threatened us),
cautious of getting too close. I don't
want to distance myself. I want
to shout, to break things, to fall

on my knee—for the man who is
only the latest (but not the last)
to die at the aggressor's knee—
for all of the named and unnamed
others. Instead I am folding the shirts
and towels. I am folding in layers
of sorrow and sorting out rage.
I am leaning into the chanting
marchers. I am folding and sorting,
singing my troubled heart,
soothing my weary soul.

ROAD TRIP BINGO

Megan Lloyd Joiner

We found her in the driveway
playing road trip bingo
with what she could see from there.

Her father took her gently by the hand
and walked her up and down the street.
She showed me her success
BINGO!

I hid my tears from her.
I've lost track of the days.

THE AMULET

Joanne M. Giannino

It's been ten days since I've put on earrings.

Today I put on these
squares of Connemara marble from Ireland,
dusty green with tree-bark brown veins,
wrapped in pewter
tied in Celtic knots.

An amulet
from my grandmother,
an amulet
from all my grandparents
who lived through
the 1918 flu pandemic.

Is there an amulet
giving you strength today?

DÓNDE ESTOY: THIS IKEA TABLE FROM ANDO THAT IS NOW A DESK

Cassandra Montenegro

Each day is a dining room table—
oak-patterned finish barely visible
below the stacks and scraps of papers
and errant caps, laptop emerging from
this mass of mischief, the pitfalls
and pearls of productivity.

What would it take for me to step away
from it—from the too-full agenda
that dictates my days, to the point that
taking the time to clean this mess
is a luxury I cannot afford?

What if I look at this disorder,
this disarray, as a disguise that belies
some truth about the real order of things?
What if I gently, gingerly accepted
that what is is not always what will be?

That sometimes you need to leave one
mess in order to make progress on another.
That what we need to keep us afloat in
the moment isn't what we'll need tomorrow.
That just because it looks like a mess
doesn't mean that there really is one.

And just because you needed to let go
or hold onto something to survive, doesn't
mean that you won't decide in a moment's time
that you are now ready to get up
and shelve these books to make space
for others.

THE PEOPLE ON THE STREET

Lisa Doege

Some years ago, I listened as several nuns reminisced about being young in the convent. It seems Easter Monday was a highlight of the year—the day they were encouraged to walk the streets of town in pairs so that they might encounter Jesus on the road to Emmaus.

As I write on Easter Monday of 2020, I think of those once-young nuns, equally eager to see Jesus in the faces of the people they met and to simply be outside the walls of the convent. Who can't relate to that second eagerness today, as we are discouraged from leaving the walls of our confinement? Cautioned to keep apart if we do venture forth. Advised to consider (how's that for ambivalent guidance?) wearing masks. How, under such conditions, are we to encounter Jesus? How are we to recognize the human face of the divine in others when we are staying at home, physically distancing, and masking ourselves for the greater good?

A familiar *Sesame Street* bit asks, "Who are the people in your neighborhood?" and answers, "They're the people that you meet when you're walking down the street. They're the people that you meet each day." Well then, if we're not walking down the street or meeting anyone each day, does that mean we no longer have a neighborhood? On the one hand, that's a nonsensical rhetorical question. But on the other hand, it, along with the question about how we are to notice the divine in human form, is the existential question of this time: how are we to be good neighbors when our ingrained means of doing so are now dangerous?

We stay home, away from physical human contact, because humans *do* embody the image of God and *are* too precious to risk infecting. We don't walk down the street, meeting neighbors, teachers, letter carriers, shopkeepers, clerks or anyone else, because we want so very much, when this is all over, to see them all alive and well.

You've heard this all a hundred times over the past four or five weeks. It's still hard, isn't it? Maybe it would help to think of the stay-at-home order as Opposite Time. We declare our neighborliness, we bow before the spark of the holy in everyone, by doing the opposite of all the ways we used to show care for one another. And thus we live to see the day when handshakes and hugs and kisses connect us again, heart and soul and sacred body. And masks are removed to reveal again our beloved glory.

BIRTHING

Kim Wildszewski

It's true that I did not carry you in my own womb.
I did not bear or bite down to bring you into this world.
But I held you as you were released from it
and cradled you in the folds of my body each night before.

I bear your absence.
And bite back at the dragon of my grief
when it looks to take me too.

I didn't want to see the end of summer;
a season between us.
But the hurricanes are here.
The mourning doves are crying.

Here is the stick.
Hear the labor pangs.

FACES OF GRIEF

Holly Mueller

Grief wears so many faces.
We will not open the door to her as sadness,
so she kicks it down as anger
filling your chest with fire for all who pass.
We will not recognize her as loss,
so she cloaks herself in numbness,
inviting us to screens and bottles and escape hatches
    with no escape.
We won't speak to her as fear,
so she whispers that we're powerless, that it's pointless,
    that we're stuck.

We won't look at her on the news
or acknowledge her waiting in our bedrooms,
so we live a life so small we don't think that she can
    enter it.
But she can.
She does.
She did.
She is uninvited
but not unkind.
She wants to clean your wounds despite the sting,
hear your memories despite the tears
paint you pictures of what was
and what could be.

A LETTER TO THOSE WE LOST TOO SOON

Mya Sophia Wade-Harper

For you, I smile when I am broken
For you, I ask for strength as the white woman
questions my words
For you, I ask for patience when the Black woman
thinks I am not Black enough
For you, I speak
For you, I bear the pain of trying
For you, I do the in-between work so that I can
tell our history
For you, I do what I can for our freedom
For you, I pray
For though I did not know you personally, I know
some of your pain
I hear our ancestors stirring in the roar of the
protests
I see my people's bodies broken and trying
I feel the fear that maybe today the world will not
see me as human
You are a part of us, we are connected as one
As one human race
And so I do this for you
I write this for you, for the life lost

I shout when the world wants me to be quiet
I laugh with joy when all I want to do is cry
I learn, I educate, I care for myself and others, I live
This will be my resistance

It is all for you
And our people

BLESSING OF THE EMOTIONAL SUPPORT ANIMALS

Ebony C. Peace

Blessed are the emotional support animals in our lives. We feed and care for them. They feed us with their unconditional love.

Blessed are the emotional support animals. In our darkest moments, when no words could ever soothe our pain, they speak to us with their body language: purring, licking, chirping, following us around, barking at us in joy.

Blessed are the emotional support animals who sit or lie on us in supportive silence. Holding us with their little claws, paws, or scales in sacred, safe space.

When we prayed for the pain to end, the Spirit of Life said—they did not cause our pain. Reminded us we are often victimized by other imperfect humans. By our own imperfect decisions. By existing in an imperfect world where it is impossible for ourselves or loved ones to live forever in good health and vitality. Where the natural circle of life reigns supreme.

Blessed are they who are our light in our darkest hour, our blanket in the coldest night, a joyful distraction from life's pain. The gift of gifts. The epitome of unconditional love. How can our emotional support animals be anything but holy?

Blessed are the emotional support animals who teach us how to love and care for ourselves again.

Blessed are they who kept us sane when we—or our surroundings—felt crazy. Who kept us alive when we wished to end. May we cherish, honor, and thank the Blessed Radiance for bringing them into our lives.

Blessed are the emotional support animals who have transitioned to the next stage of being. They wait for us, forever faithful. In love. In holiness.

WHAT NOW?

Roger Butts

Pray for the one who is angry at God.
His wife is upstairs in critical care, basically alone,
being loved by nurses and docs and chaplains
the best we can. She will die and he knows it.
If praying is your thing, go ahead and pray.

There is another one today whose loved one is dying.
He too is mad. He's mad at the doctors for not trying
the latest recommendation from this president,
which is no kind of cure, no kind of treatment.
Sometimes, grief looks like lashing out at anything and
    anyone.

Keep him in your heart, if that is your thing.
Hold him in the Light. Thank a nurse,
if you'd like to do something a bit more concrete.

People ask me: Where have you seen the holy in this
    Covid-madness?
Once, approaching midnight, a nurse lovingly helped a
    woman put on
her PAPR, knowing this would be the last time she saw
    her husband alive.
Later, the nurse took it off. The grieving, lost wife looked
    at me
and said: Chaplain, what more should I have done?
    What now?

What now? It is the only question, the most important
   thing.
Bring solace where you can in the way you can.
Bring a word of consolation, sing a song of hope.
Sit in silence and hold in your heart's hands the angry one,
the grieving one, the lost one, the sick one, the left behind.

A long time ago, my loving uncle visited my family in
   Colorado.
My seven-year-old, shy, hid behind a chair. His smile
   brought her out.
As he was leaving, he said: Norah, God has great things
   in store for you.
She never forgot it. *What now?* Bless a child, and then
   another.

There is pain in this world and there is loss. There are
   tears upon tears.
So too is there hope. So too is there a blessing, never
   forgotten.
Keep choosing to bless the world. Before Covid-19, the
   world needed love.
Your love. Your peace. Your blessing. During and after,
   the world needs
you, just as you are, just as you are becoming, to bless it
   and keep it in your heart.

*I have blessed you so that you might be a blessing to each and
   everyone. Genesis 12*

PRAYER SIN ORACIÓN

Cassandra Montenegro

Written for the South Florida Unitarian Universalist
People of Color and Indigenous Gathering

Today, on this National Day of Prayer, may we pray for the lives lost to this virus, and the lives born amidst it. For the hurt and anger, the joy and comfort.

To those for whom prayer is a painful word to hear, may we pray without prayer—orando sin oración—with our individual and collective action toward justice.

Together, may we redefine and reclaim the place and power of prayer.

MAKING MASKS

Amanda K. Poppei

It made sense in the beginning, I guess.

They (whoever "they" is—the WHO, the CDC, some longform article in the *Atlantic*) had just told us that actually we *should* be wearing masks. It was early days, and you couldn't buy a mask to save your life. In a month you'd be able to order masks with your favorite cartoon characters and sports teams and presidential candidates on them, but back then people were wrapping bandanas around their faces and pulling up turtlenecks.

The *New York Times* published a guide to making your own mask, and suddenly I knew why I had been hoarding quilting fabric for years without any actual knowledge of quilting. I had a sewing machine. I had the fabric. I had a measuring tape. Surely I could do this.

My first few attempts were a bit crooked. It took a while to figure out what kind of elastic worked best. I went through an ill-fated phase of trying to use pipe cleaners for nose pieces. But all in all, I was right: I could do this. Once there were enough for my family, I made them for my uncle, who lived alone and isolated. For my parents, who were only leaving the house once every two weeks for groceries. For my friend down the block, who wasn't at all handy with a needle.

The mask-making industry took off around me, and at some point it became clear that I could buy masks everywhere from Target to Etsy . . . and honestly, they probably would have been better made and a better use of money, if you really counted the cost of my time. But once I had started, I found I couldn't stop. I didn't want to. I fit the sewing into odd times of day, cutting and pinning fabric one afternoon and adding the elastic the next morning. I perfected the size my older child liked and made sure she had as many bright colors as her heart desired. I figured out a different way to do the elastic so it didn't rub against my younger daughter's ears. I offered the ones that were too small for anyone in our family on the neighborhood listserv. I made some for my in-laws when they finally accepted that Covid was going to be here for a while. I reached deeper into my fabric stash, planning which patterns would be nice to bring out once the weather turned cold. I perfected the art of re-threading the bobbin. I learned what those error messages on my sewing machine meant. I could do this.

And ultimately, of course, that's the thing: I could do this. There is so little I can do right now. So little that will make much of a difference at all. But I can cut and pin and sew. I can make these little double-layered pieces of cloth that protect my family and the world. Whenever I sit down at my machine, I feel the line stretching back to the sewers before me, to the women who planted Victory gardens, to all those who have cut up scraps and shared seeds with their neighbors and taken what they had around them to fashion . . . something. Something that would grow, or protect, or survive.

Maybe someday we'll want a fancy mask, or one with perfect embroidery or a high-tech filter. For now, when I see my children's eyes peeking above the brightly colored fabric with its uneven stitches, I think: I can do this. We can do this. And I pull out the fabric pile and the straight pins again.

PRAYER FOR WHILE IN THE STRUGGLE

Margalie Belizaire

Spirit of light and love,
Spirit of resistance,
Spirit of generosity,
That which serves as our conscience in this work
That we do to dismantle white supremacy,
To empower the marginalized,
To insist that Black lives matter:
We have been angered.
We have been saddened.
We have been pushed to the brink once more.
We are inspired and resolved to do better this time.
To not simply get to the other side of this moment,
But to get there morally healthier.
To get to a safer space for Black bodies.
Spirit, help us to understand that we each have a role in
    justice work,
For our liberations are tied to one another's.
Give us the clarity of mind to know what our individual
    part is in the struggle.
That there are many ways to protest injustice.
Help us to find our way and commit to it.
Spirits, we ask for guidance.
Send us strength and endurance.
Help us to give our all to this
And hold nothing back,

For precious lives depend on it.

We will be imperfect.

Rest assured that we will mess up over and over again

And we must do it anyway.

May we summon the courage to tear down this system
    of injustice

And get busy creating a "world community with . . .
    justice for all."

May it be so.

Amen.

F*** YOU

Manish Mishra-Marzetti

You,
these systems and structures
I did not design,
    that were imposed on my
        Ancestors,
    that my immigrant parents believed
        held the keys to security and happiness;

You,
    who convinced me in my youth,
    amidst the images of blue-eyed
        Captain Kirk
    and fair-haired Luke Skywalker,
    that I am not the Ideal
        of Beauty, or Courage, or Strength
        or anything really;

You,
    who continuously spindle and weave
    new tricks,
    new patterns,
    of control and dominance:

If I name my pain,
    I am a sad sack
        bumming you out;

If I reject your ways of forcefully embodying
    power and authority,
        patterns of hierarchy and domination,
    I am weak
        and don't know how to lead;
If I ask for a shared spotlight,
    equal ability to showcase my
        Art, Creativity, and Wisdom,
    you cry and bemoan your loss
        of central and exclusive focus.

You,
    who one grandfather fought against,
    and another tried to work with,

You—white supremacy
        western hegemony
        colonialist arrogance
        capitalistic greed,
you reside in me.
How could you not?
I am a child of your civilization
    even as I strive to be
        more
    than what you are.

Many children have the day when
    they reject
        that which birthed them,
        that which they have outgrown,

as they struggle and seek
to forge—independence
        voice
        perspective
        a path.

You are in me.
You are bound through generations
    to my lineage.
And
    I reject you.

I am more than you.
My power, my voice, my wisdom
    are mine to claim.

PSALM 121: WE LIFT UP OUR WEARY EYES

Ali Bell-Delgado

We lift up our eyes to the hills—
from where will our help come?
God of our understanding, hear our prayers
Where do we find help in these sorrowful times?
We are seeking something to hold us.
Someone to hold us, we for we feel so weary.
Tired of the way that this virus is infecting our loved
    ones. Sickening some and stealing others.
Tired of the murderous rage of racism that is being used
    as a tool of execution against Black and brown bodies.
We are so weary.
Tired of worrying about how we will survive day after
    day in this pandemic.
Tired of worrying if we are preparing our children for
    this world that they have inherited.
We are so weary.
Tired of feeling isolated in our homes.
Tired of not being able to greet each other with hugs
    and handshakes.
We are so weary.
From where will our help come?
We lift our weary eyes.
Spirit of Life,
We beseech you.
Help us to dig deeper into our faith.

Not the faith of fairytales and limited understanding.

Not the faith that these things will change somehow
without our doing the work of change.

Help us to dig deeper into our faith in humanity.

We know that we have all that we need to fundamentally
change these things:

Racism.

If we do the work of dismantling the system of white
supremacy in our world, in our community, in our
churches, congregations, and fellowships, in our
homes, and in ourselves.

The spread of this pandemic.

If we continue to hold the line against a government
that places profit above lives.

Survival.

If we remind ourselves that if we have, we need to give.
If we need, we can trust our community and ask
for help.

We know we are all a part of the interdependent web.
Each of us needing and each of us giving. That
interdependence keeps us connected and makes us
stronger.

The education of our children.

If we remember that, just like each of us, children strive
to do justice, to love fully, to seek truth. Remind us
that to truly protect them, we must be forthright in
our telling of these events.

Our isolation from community.

If we remember that we have each other, we can depend on the web to hold us. Remind us that our bodies have stored the sensation of touches that have brought us joy and comfort. Remind us to wrap ourselves in this touch when we are missing each other. For we are right here (head), right here (heart), right here (hug).

We are the keepers of each other; we are our shade and we are our healing light.

We are the keepers of each other; we are our aid and we are our salvation.

We are the keepers of each other; we are the weavers and we are the web.

May we remember.

May we act.

May it be so.

Ashe, Amen.

DUCKLINGS

Holly Mueller

One morning in late April, I was greeted by tiny, fluffy ducklings when I arrived at the inpatient hospice where I am a chaplain. Our hospice unit is built around a secluded green courtyard, so it made sense that a mother duck had chosen that safely enclosed spot in which to guard and hatch her babies.

At the time, we had recently started admitting Covid-positive patients to our facility. We were struggling with whether to allow visitors, wanting to mitigate risk and also not wanting patients to die apart from their families. How could we keep ourselves and our patients safe without compounding the trauma of loss with separation at the end of life?

And so, in the midst of weighing difficult value choices and managing our own anxiety, small feathery beings greeted us every morning. And I do mean every morning. There was no way to get to out of the courtyard except by flight, so Mama Duck was now trapped in our courtyard with eight flightless babies. We were reluctant to usher wild ducklings through the building to reach the wider world, so we had to wait for them to fledge. Our director bought a baby pool and duck food, and the ducklings spent their days splashing in their inflatable pool under the watchful eye of their mother.

We were all charmed. The patients and their loved ones, able to see the avian family from their rooms, watched with delight. As the days passed, they grew bigger, still waddling after their mother and spending the increasingly warm afternoons in their little duckling spa. It wasn't just that they were cute and that we enjoyed providing sanctuary for such fragile beings—the ducklings gave us moments throughout the day when we were not healthcare providers in a pandemic. They let us focus on birth instead of the death we were facing; they filled us with awe just by daring to exist with such wild, ordinary, cute abandon. They were like winged meditations just outside our windows.

But the mama duck felt no such awe. She started waiting by the doors of the courtyard hoping to lead her ducklings out. As the days grew hotter, she became more upset that she and her children were stuck. She had kept her babies safe, but at the cost of being trapped.

As the weeks wore on, our distress grew with hers. The safe, anxious, isolated ducks were an all-too-obvious mirror for our own experience. How long would this last? How do we protect each other? How do we survive?

Once the ducklings were able to fly away, I found myself still looking out in the courtyard in the mornings, surprised not to find their fluffy little wings waiting for me. Unlike the ducklings, our escape from the isolation, fear, and grief of the pandemic will not be so soon or concrete. As we navigate the long, messy road to safety and freedom, it is easy to feel like the seriousness of the pandemic means we should remain hyper-focused and respectfully somber. But our duckling guests taught me to take my eyes off that road sometimes. They showed me the necessity of making space for moments of peace and delight within our larger struggles, to be open to the ordinary wonder and surprising companions that waddle across our path.

DOING ALRIGHT

Alix Klingenberg

I'm pretty sure we're doing alright,
even though we're always late
and the food comes prepared
and you watch more TV than I ever imagined.

I'm pretty sure I'm enough,
even though I've worn the same
sweatshirt for six days straight
and I can't seem to clean the bedroom
or unpack the boxes of books.

I'm pretty sure you'll be ok,
even though you don't act like other kids
and transitions make you cranky
and you spend most of your life daydreaming.

I'm pretty sure there's no right way to do this thing,
this family life endeavor,
except to be in it every day, and to
laugh and try to be yourself in every way you know how . . .

Even if it means I hide away in the bathroom,
writing poetry on my phone
while the puppy sleeps
and you eat hummus straight from the container with a
    spoon.

Pretty sure we're doing alright.

DANDELION KINDNESS

Fiona Heath

Many of us are living with some level of fear and stress
and frustration and anxiety. These are difficult times—
a fragile democracy, systemic racism, pandemics, the
climate crisis—all of which impact our health, our work,
and our lives. Most of us are in some way struggling to
survive.

In the hard times, kindness between people is needed
and necessary.

As people of the chalice, kindness is the lived expression of the principles we hold dear. Being kind to ourselves
affirms our own value even when others would deny it.
Acts of kindness toward others show that they have value
and worth outside of any moment or relationship.

Kindness also roots us in the seventh principle, the
understanding of our interdependence. We are deeply
connected to all other life on earth. The Covid-19 pandemic has shown the intricate weaving of human bonds.
We are all in this together.

I think of this kindness, the kindness that requires
us to dig deep and unearth our resiliency, as dandelion
kindness.

If you have seen a patch of grass in spring, you know
that dandelions are tenacious. Mow them down and
they spring back up. Their roots go down, deep down—
you can rip out the stems and tear off the leaves, and

with time the dandelion will once more bloom a cheerful yellow.

Dandelion kindness—kindness that wells up in the face of all challenges—is what we need.

We get torn down and we grow back up. We face our struggles and we help each other survive. Dandelion kindness does not mean we are going to be kind all the time in every moment—no perfect people here! It means we return, again and again, to kindness as our baseline.

A BLESSING FOR THOSE WHOSE LOVED ONE WAS NOT PERFECT

Lora Brandis

Bless you whose loved one was not perfect.
Bless you whose dear departed didn't find the cure for
    cancer or free the people.
Bless you who when people say, "you have your
    memories to comfort you,"
remain silent and smile anyway.
Bless you who knew loss before your loved one died.
Bless you who watched your loved one die over time.
Bless you who lost your loved one suddenly.
Bless you who were not there.
Bless you who witnessed the trauma at home or in a
    hospital.
Bless you who cling to the memories of a loved one who
    was not perfect
because loving them was the greatest gift they gave you.
Bless you who will love them always.
Bless you in your grief and your loss and your mourning
    and your heartbreak.
Bless you.

PRAYER FOR THE LAMP KEEPER

Joe Cherry

My prayer for you today is that you understand that you cannot be and say everything. That you are a light, a lamp in the night to help people find their way, but you cannot be their way.

Remember also that a steady lamp by which others may guide their own journey is a gift from and to the universe.

Be steady, but do not deny your own humanity. Do not forget to take breaks. Do not let your desire to be that steward of that lamp keep you too long from your own journey.

Share the burden.
Share the responsibility.
Share the honor with others.

NEW MOTHER OF THE PANDEMIC

Alyssa Franklin

I am a new mother
of the pandemic.
Please give me patience;
I know no other experience
of how to mother
except one of
fear, disease,
dis-ease, distance,
and unknowns.

I am a new mother
of the pandemic.
Please give me grace
as I clutch my babe
tighter to my chest.
My little family
is all I touch
For 136 days
and counting:
a promise of protection,
a mark of privilege.

I am a new mother
of the pandemic.
Please give me care.
They say new motherhood

is isolating,
and some days I feel isolated
inside of isolation.
My own mother
cannot hug me
congratulations.

I am a new mother
of the pandemic.
Please give me strength.
Decisions weigh heavy on my mind
every part of every day:
Who to see?
What to do?
What is best?
How do I know?

I am a new mother
of the pandemic.
I try to give myself space
to hold all of this
fear, questioning, pride,
anxiety, love, anger, hope . . .

I am a new mother
of the pandemic,
grappling with the fragility of mortality
and the fullness of new life
in the same breath.

WITH YOU

Linnea Nelson

Neither you nor I wanted to be apart
for your journey to the unknown.
I always, always thought
I would be there to hold you close
as you took your last breath—
sitting beside you,
bowing down with
    tears rolling down my face.

I wish comfort for you
in these final hours.
May you feel loved.
May you feel peace.

Yet here I am,
and you are there.
I touch my heart and,
yes, right there!
You must know—
our hearts beat in time,
for I am with you.

QUIET BRAVERY

Holly Mueller

It was early in the pandemic when I got the call to
go visit a family on a Thursday evening. I work as a
chaplain with a hospice company, which often involves
making house calls. The house was overflowing, family
members who couldn't fit inside spilling onto the front
porch. The patient was just being enrolled in hospice and
was already declining quickly, so the extended family
had gathered in force. No one in the family wore a mask,
and it was so early in the pandemic that my company
wasn't yet providing them. And so it was with some
trepidation that I entered the crowded home, listening to
stories of the patient's life, praying at her bedside, holding
the grief of so many children and grandchildren. I tried
to keep my distance, but didn't yet have the vocabulary
for turning down hugs, for backing away.

Several hours later, when I had done what I could,
I said my goodbyes and got into my car. As I turned off
their street onto the main road, I began to cry. Not for
the family, nor the patient I had just blessed, but for how
very vulnerable I felt, going into crowded homes in the
middle of a pandemic. I was scared, and my tears turned
to hiccupping sobs as I got on the highway. I have never
been a particularly brave person. I have to psych myself
up to engage in conflict resolution; I prefer my risks to be
very calculated; I never even liked the high dive as a kid.

And suddenly, bravery was not a choice. I couldn't climb back down the ladder. I couldn't decide this conflict wasn't worth it. Short of deconstructing the life I'd built and quitting my vocation, this had become my life. It was bravery or bust.

At first, a hot, panicky feeling followed me through my days. As we learned more, my work took more steps to protect its employees, working by phone when possible and wearing masks and face shields when it was not. And over time, the hot panicky feeling subsided. It was replaced with a feeling of grit. I became a chaplain to make meaning, to walk with people in their grief, to be present with them when it was too painful for many to stay by their side. My vulnerability to the pandemic was just the cost of following that call.

And inside that grit there was a quieter posture, a gentle, mundane rhythm of survival. Humans adapt; humans have survived and are surviving much worse things than I am, and they keep going. They keep living. The get up and eat what food they have and do the work that is at hand and love those around them as well as they can. We are fed by the strength of another sunrise and another one after that.

All my cautious life, I had thought bravery was a splashy, daring choice. I thought it was loud and dangerous and reserved for only the foolhardiest among us. Each time I froze in a crisis or stayed safely on the sidelines, I lamented the cowardice I offered the world. But

I've found that there is a quieter bravery—the kind that finds you instead of you finding it, the kind that just asks you to show up each day and do what you can and then put yourself to bed so you can do it again. It is that quiet bravery I have found inside myself that has let me do what the world and my values ask of me every single day.

PRAYER FOR MAY 31, 2020, IN MINNEAPOLIS, SIX DAYS AFTER THE POLICE KILLED GEORGE FLOYD

Arif Mamdani and Ruth MacKenzie

READER A: Spirit of Life and Love, God of freedom and fire

READER B: Breath of life that flowed through my ancestors. One whom my grandmother knew, and knelt, and prayed to.

READER B: There are truths that we don't speak in mixed company. Things that we don't say. Things that we won't say unless we know that those receiving our words are trustworthy.

READER A: Deliver us from assuming that justice-making is gentle or orderly. We have been living in a land of bondage whether we recognize it or not.

Here in the land of Egypt,

READER B: Here in a land like ours, sometimes the only space we speak the truth

is in the silence of our hearts.

READER A: Here in the land of Black lives snuffed out day in and day out, on camera, on a busy street, or in a bedroom . . .

- READER A: we cry out
- READER B: we cry out with grocery carts flung against the barricades

- READER B: we cry out in Zoom meetings
- READER A: we cry out with posters and raised fists
- READER A: we cry out while the fires rage and buildings fall
- READER B: we cry out for our children—our black, our brown, our white children
- READER A: we cry out and bring food
- READER A: we cry out and bear witness
- READER A: we cry out with brooms and trash bags to pick up the refuse from all the prayers strewn across the city streets from the night before

READER B: Here in this space of silence, we give voice to what we really feel.

What we truly feel
- is rage
- is a longing for the sharp knives of judgment to be wielded
- for justice to cut out the heart of white supremacy
- to cut out a system that takes our breath away.

READER A: We have cried so many tears that our throats are raw and hope of a promised land is all but gone. It's the same story, over and over, again and again, and nothing seems to change.

READER B: The bended knee to the powers that be. Worshiping capitalism and white supremacy.

READER A: Some of us have been conditioned to turn away

READER A: Egypt is comfortable and advantageous

READER B: Some of us are buckling under the weight of the knee on our necks

READER B: Some of us can't breathe

READER A: Some of us are confused

READER A: Some of us are steadfast

READER B: Some of us are scared

READER B: Some of us are angry

READER A: Some of us are numb

READER A: Some of us are rageful

READER B: Our sorrow brings us to our knees.

This has been happening for as long as our ancestors had breath to tell us their stories.

Our Black and brown and queer bodies brutalized by the state

These tears have been flowing for generations and they flow still

READER A: But here we are in the midst of the fires, aching for a way forward.

We pray:

READER B: Breath of life. God of my ancestors.

Help us to give voice to the scream of rage and pain and frustration that has been building and building and building for so long.

READER A: Spirit of Life and Love, propel us into a new Exodus

We only need a few essential things for the journey:

- a loaf of bread to share
- a hand to hold
- a willingness to follow the covenant we repeat every Sunday

READER B: To welcome, affirm, and protect the light in each human heart.

READER A: To listen deeply to where Love is calling us next.

READER B: To work for justice with humility, bravery, and compassion.

READER A: And commit our lives to racial justice.

READER B: On this morning, our hearts aching and exhausted,

READER A: We name our fears, our concerns, our confusion, our anger, and our sadness.

READER B: These are times of curfew and quarantine. Rage and sorrow. And these are also times of surprising grace, moments when the breath of life breaks through in new ways and transforms our lives with meaning and the promise of a world that could be.

READER A: May the grip of addiction be loosened

READER B: May the weight of oppression be lightened

READER A: May grief be shared

READER B: May joy break through and may love make every suffering bearable for us all.

READERS A AND B: Amen.

Note: This prayer was offered as part of the Sunday service on May 31, 2020, at First Universalist Church of Minneapolis. As such, it incorporates language that is part of our regular liturgy. The affirmations ("To welcome, affirm, and protect . . .") were written by the Ministers and Program Directors of First Universalist Church, and the prayer closing ("May the grip of addiction be loosened . . .") was written by Reverend Jen Crow.

SORROW

Linnea Nelson

My sorrow is unbound,
streaming outward in all directions.

I want to curl up on the sofa,
my head and body
under a blanket,
to feel it all,
there in the dark
where no one can see me.

I'll capture the sorrow
and keep it close to me.

I need to feel unbound for a while.

FEAR

Megan Lloyd Joiner

I would like to speak eloquently about fear
But I do not know what to say
Except that we are becoming accustomed to it.

Everyone—even those we love—is a threat

A potential risk
A possible death sentence.

We cross the street.
We usher the children away.
Six feet is beginning to feel not far enough

We are alone
and afraid.

GIFT OF LIFE

Erica L. Barlett

I didn't realize the extent of my pandemic grief until I
stumbled across a packet of papers about my aunt Gail's
death by suicide.

Up until then, I'd been in denial, trying to act like
the pandemic wasn't impacting me much. After all, I
have a job I can easily do from home. I don't have kids
to support through the challenges of virtual education.
My dad is healthy and doesn't need caregiving. I live in
Maine with access to many beautiful outdoor spots.

But when I looked at that packet, now fourteen years
old, things shifted, especially when I read the Gift of
Life letter. It details how my aunt's organs improved the
lives of five other people, including two infants.

This letter has often brought me comfort, but this
time I started wondering about how those people were
managing the pandemic. Were they okay? How were the
infants—now teenagers—coping with the disruptions to
high school? Were they more at risk because they had
organ transplants? Did they, like me, feel cut off from
the world?

That's when I started crying. The tears weren't only
for me, or my lost aunt, or the people who still carried part of her. The tears were for everyone feeling

alone and disconnected. Everyone who's lost a loved one during this time but couldn't be with them at the end. Everyone who was already struggling with mental health issues, now forced into a time of isolation and uncertainty.

Only when my tears stopped could I acknowledge the reality of my grief and the reasons why I've felt so lethargic, as if there wasn't much point to anything.

Although I'm fortunate in many ways, I haven't given or received a hug since early March. I've only seen my family once. I miss church—singing hymns, chatting during coffee hour, seeing the kids during the Time for All Ages. I'm saddened by the fact that I can't get together with friends without worrying if it's dangerous. And I'm desperately tired of the uncertainty, of not knowing when all this will end.

Letting myself acknowledge and express those feelings didn't make them go away, but they did help me feel lighter. The world looked a little brighter again.

Since then, I've been thinking more about my aunt Gail and wishing I could have gotten to know her better as an adult, particularly since I'm now the age she was when she died. I feel like I'd understand her much better than I did when I was thirty.

I no longer have the chance to connect with her, but I can make other choices. To reach out more to people I care about. To let myself acknowledge the sorrow in our current situation, but also to find moments of joy.

To ask for help when I need it. To practice kindness and compassion.

When I spotted a rainbow the other day, it felt like my own gift of life, and a reminder to embrace that life while I can.

WAVES

Anne Barker

The first wave came with urgency
A sudden knowing
That everything must change.

We wouldn't take no for an answer
We must all act differently
Stop the danger
Prevent the harm.

And some of us
—So many of us—
Thought that it could be ok
Things were different now
We knew better
It's the right thing
Do it for the vulnerable
(*everyone is vulnerable.*)

Until we noticed
One by one
That it wasn't different
(*those in danger always knew—this isn't news—*
   nobody is ever safe until we all are in the game—
   Nobody.)

That first wave never ended
Just our imagining
That things would be ok.

The next wave is the critical one
Where we decide
That dying—for any reason—is not a wager
We can justly entertain
For anyone but ourselves.

ONE LITTLE LIGHT

Brenda Cole

It is strange to be looking so hard for one small light
amid oceans of loneliness, grief, and fear. Early spring
of 2020 should have been a time of joy—I had plans
to attend five family birthdays, play in our state Senior
Olympics, and travel to visit friends. But then the deaths
started and the stay-at-home orders went out.

Instead, there have been five months and counting of
staying home and staying away from my son and loved
ones. Making masks for family, losing my job, and cutting every corner to make my unemployment benefits
stretch to cover the essentials.

Desperate not to spiral into despair, I sought
moments of light—any tiny source of light, no matter
how feeble.

It started with a friend on the West Coast. She was
in lockdown with an awful job, but she sent a picture
of her large, not-too-intelligent cat trying to bat at a
bird through the window. He was so confused when he
couldn't reach it that I had to smile.

Then my grown son began to call just to chat. About
work, about the latest large animal on his place up in the
mountains, about his vocal displeasure about the dissolv-
ing of our country. I eventually smiled and even laughed.
Then I started reaching out to elderly friends to check
in with them. I heard about their pets, the humming-

birds outside their windows, and how their gardens were growing. I started opening my heart again.

I am a retired science teacher; I understand just how deadly this mismanaged pandemic may become. I wear a mask, distance, and wash until it feels as if I've scoured off entire layers of my skin. My family and friends take every precaution, and we all spend most of our time at home.

But even if the worst happens and someone I love dies from this virus, I have hope. I am a Pagan Unitarian Universalist, which means I believe that death is simply a transition to another stage of life. Those I love, whether they have already passed over or someday will, are never lost to me.

So I do my best to stay calm and help however I can. Whether listening to a friend, dropping off groceries for my son, or teaching my path to our small Pagan community, I still look for the light in everything I do.

That's why I am up way too early on this July morning, 4:45 am to be exact. I'm outside an hour before dawn looking up for a source of light—a ball of ice with a massive tail. So far the clouds have been determined to hide it; it's monsoon season here in New Mexico, and the sky is overcast. I haven't had any luck looking west after sunset either. But still, I will always look for the light.

SURVIVOR'S FAITH

Emily DeTar Birt

Before the world ended,
fires engulfed Australia.
Wombats burrowed to safety,
letting other animals take
shelter in their dens.

All my life I was taught
faith was hope.
What do wombats know of hope?
They know how to
stay alive.

Sacred ashes
whisper the names of
generations who ushered
each other underground:

to survive anyway
to love anyway
to build anyway.

Hope is a footnote.
Life is the goal.
Whatever God you believe in
wants first and foremost
for all of us to live.

SOME DAYS

Anne Barker

Some days
The exquisite brilliance of a lime
Is all it really takes.

IT IS A GOOD DAY

Danielle Di Bona

It is a good day.

Breathe . . . Take a breath and feel the weight of the
world lift from your body.

Remember . . . Remember that you survived—no,
thrived.

Find your deep soul, hold it in your hands, and thank it.
Thank that soul for its protection and power.

We have survived. We are not the same, yet we have
survived, battered and bruised.

It is a good day.

Breathe. Take a breath and feel the weight of the world
lift from your body. Let your heart be filled with
peace.

Let us each, in our own way, offer thanks to that which
is most holy for its protection and love.

Amen.

THE SHORES OF HOPE

Daniel C. Kanter

Arriving on these shores of hope, abandon your cynicism, your despair, your short view of humanity, and look up and see that we are not alone in our separateness. We are not forsaken or forlorn; we can be each other's dreams unrestrained by desperation.

We can see beyond the horizon of setbacks and defeat and know that others have journeyed farther than we have. They have seen so much and not lost themselves to resignation.

Arriving on these shores of hope, embrace the here and now, the blessings and the presence of holy matters. Here, now, we are together and we are stronger for it. Whether you are forlorn or uplifted, let us together enter worship as if it was a new matter, a new day, a new chance at life.

ALL SOULS DAY

Steven Leigh Williams

Holy Breath:
    We cannot breathe.
Holy Tears:
    We are cried out.
Holy Sobs:
    Our ragged gasps and tearless weeping.

You, Beloved, are still alive.
Yours is not to wonder why—

not why, but how
your cries may breathe life
into this world of the dying.

For so long as we live there
is hope for reprieve
and restoration.

Ours is not to wonder why.
We, Beloved, are still alive.

Holy Sobs:
    Our prayers of lamentation.
Holy Tears:
    Our baptismal font.

Holy Breath:
    Our inspiration.
        Draw us home
            to the kin-dom
                of our co-creation.

SABBATH

Megan Lloyd Joiner

I lock the door behind me
My heart sleeps inside

I am afraid
of what is coming

And what we have already lost
Be still my heart

Rest this day
To comfort is to make strong

Unlock the door.

SOLSTICE: LITANY FOR THE LONG DARKNESS

Atena O. Danner

I will not meet darkness with fear in my heart
I will breathe in peace and breathe out fear
Breathe in curiosity and breathe out fear
Breathe in growth and breathe out fear
Breathe in patience and breathe out
Fear of the dark, which does not serve me.

I cast out the binaries of dark/light: wrong/right
I cast out that false naming
I watch and wait for the longest dark night
I cherish the blessing of the long, dark night
I await my return to the longest, darkest night.

You, who taught me stillness . . .
You, who gave me depth . . .
You, who held me the longest, and hold me still . . .

I return to you, darkness, again and again
Dissolve into the deep to be made myself
Nurtured by your very nature

Gratefully, humbly, I return
Renewed in your healing touch.

THE TURNING

QuianaDenae Perkins

At the last turning, I was invited to a meeting among
the sun,
the earth, and
the moon.

The sun asked, "Do you have space in your heart for a
    great light?"
The earth said, "I will hold you down if you are willing."
The moon said, "I will guide you if you need it."

And it was easy to say *yes* to the energies of balance.
So for a turning, we have found ourselves dancing.

The sun took the lead,
sharing a drop of their luminescence.
I held it deep in my heart when the darkness loomed,
held it on the tip of my fingers when others called for it.
Coming to understand space
becoming a beacon.
Learning the nuance of shadow and light.

The earth kept her word.
I was planted deep and rooted hard.
I was uprooted, replanted, and loved until
I was healed and able to feel the small tug from soil
    calling me down,

demanding I grow
again.

And the moon, a sister auntie, stayed faithful at my side.
Always hovering,
always playing, laughing,
reminding me that joy takes many forms and keeps no
    schedule.
Reassuring me with loving pats and *oh, child!* whispered
    commentary.
A subtle and wanted companion on this journey.

And the turning is coming again.

The sun said, "Daughter, you have done well."
The earth said, "Healer, who is still healing, you always
    have home."
The moon said, "Beloved shadow worker, we will cast
    new spells soon."

We radiate the light
    We rotate the life
        We revolve back into love
            We enter a new season of possibilities.

NEW YEAR'S FLOOD

Kate Wilkinson

Four days into the New Year, our church flooded. All
week I had been writing a sermon about New Year's
resolutions. It was a good sermon; a little scientific,
maybe. It was all about how our brain works and how
that makes New Year's resolutions so hard to keep. There
was a nod to Buddhism and the practice of mindfulness.
Some recommendations by psychologists and a life coach
about making small steps toward big changes. A good,
strong ending.

Then the church flooded.

In the following days, a steady stream of volunteers
came by to see how we were doing and how they could
help. We rummaged through closets and cabinets, sorting out what was waterlogged and what was salvageable.
We spent hours on the phone with the insurance company. We taped off what wasn't safe.

I'll admit that at times the enormity of the situation
before me got overwhelming. The sheer amount of mud
and trash and soggy cardboard boxes was just too much.
And as I dried out soggy marriage licenses and threw
away dear mementos, I did get sad.

But all week I had been researching how to keep a
New Year's resolution, and the advice began sounding
in my ear. Turns out it holds just as true for floods as
resolutions:

- Do not let yourself be overwhelmed by the enormity of your goal or task. Just take the next small step.
- Do not let your emotions hook you. Use mindfulness to detach from the task before you and you will realize that flossing your teeth does not have to be arduous. Throwing things out does not have to be devastating. These can be neutral activities; they can even be joyous.
- Taken one small step at a time, goals can be reached. Insurance policies can be navigated. A challenge can become an opportunity.

Slowly the flood became an opportunity to clean out our junk, to become more selective about what we keep. To rebuild smarter and to store things higher. It was an opportunity to take stock of what was really important to us, which turned out not to be *things*.

I ended up scrapping my sermon that Sunday. But that good strong ending that I had written earlier in the week still held. So I ended my new sermon with that . . .

I saw a cartoon the other day that I loved. In the first frame, one person asks the other one, "Why so optimistic about the New Year? What do you think it will bring? Everything seems so messed up."

The second person answers, "I think it will bring flowers."

"Yeah, how come?" asks the first person.

And the second person, who is on her hands and knees in the dirt, answers, "Because I am planting flowers."

We don't know everything that the new year holds. But some of what we can expect is based on the seeds we are sowing now that will come to flower and bear fruit in time. May this be a year full of flowers. May it be a year of resolutions, of communities coming together in hard times, of weathering storms and floods and personal hurts. May it be a year in which we always remember that our best treasures are each other.

Happy New Year!

ESSENTIAL SERVICES

Michael Tino

You are essential.
Your life is essential.
Your body is essential.
Your presence, here in community, is essential.
Here, we mourn the dead.
Here, we rage at injustice.
Here, we learn and grow, stretch and challenge
    ourselves.
Here, we plan and build the beloved community.
Here, we remember what is greater than ourselves.
Here, we celebrate joyous milestones and mark the
    seasons turning.
Our work here is essential because we are essential.
Not just those of us who are here—
but all of our siblings, of every faith, color, and identity.
All of us are essential.
Come, let us worship,
connected,
whole,
essential.

THE INSPIRIT SERIES

Unitarians and Universalists have been publishing collections of prayers and meditations for more than 175 years. In 1841 the Unitarians broke with their tradition of publishing only formal theology and released *Short Prayers for the Morning and Evening of Every Day in the Week, with Occasional Prayers and Thanksgivings.* Over the ensuing years, the Unitarians published many more volumes of prayers, including Theodore Parker's selections. In 1938, *Gaining a Radiant Faith* by Henry H. Saunderson launched the tradition of an annual Lenten manual.

Several Universalist collections appeared in the early nineteenth century as well. A comprehensive *Book of Prayers* was published in 1839, featuring both public and private devotions. Like the Unitarians, the Universalists published Lenten manuals, and in the 1950s they complemented this series with Advent manuals.

In 1961, the year the Unitarians and Universalists consolidated, the Lenten manual evolved into a meditation manual. And in 2015, reflecting a renewed vision for a wider audience, the name evolved once again into the inSpirit series.

For a complete list of titles in the inSpirit series,
please visit **uua.org/inspirit**